THE BEST OF

Jane Grigson's
SOUPS

THE BEST OF

Jane Grigson's
SOUPS

50 classic recipes

Jane Grigson

MICHAEL JOSEPH
LONDON

MICHAEL JOSEPH LTD
Published by the Penguin Group
27 Wrights Lane, London W8 5TZ
Viking Penguin Inc., 375 Hudson Street, New York, New York 10014, USA
Penguin Books Australia Ltd, Ringwood, Victoria, Australia
Penguin Books Canada Ltd, 10 Alcorn Avenue, Toronto, Ontario,
Canada M4V 3B2
Penguin Books (NZ) Ltd, 182–190 Wairau Road, Auckland 10, New Zealand
Penguin Books Ltd, Registered Offices: Harmondsworth, Middlesex, England

First published in Great Britain 1993
Copyright © Sophie Grigson 1993

Illustrations by Jane Strother

Typeset by Selwood Systems, Midsomer Norton
Made and printed in England by Butler & Tanner Ltd, Frome and London
A CIP catalogue record for this book is available from the British Library

ISBN 0 7181 0042 5

The moral right of the author has been asserted

NOTE

The recipes in this book have been selected from Jane Grigson's many cookery books written over a number of years. Inevitably, therefore, the recipes vary in the amount of detailed method given and some assume knowledge of cooking techniques. If in doubt, an experienced cook will be able to use his/her own judgement; a less experienced cook will probably find enough assistance in any general cookery book.

....

QUANTITIES

Serving quantities are indicated at the beginning of each recipe, though these are intended as a general guide, and you must allow for the rest of the meal, or the position of a dish in the meal, when making your calculations.

When measuring ingredients, follow either metric or imperial systems, not a mixture. Metric measurements are given first.

STOCK

In the recipes that require stock, for the best results it is recommended that you do not use a stock cube but use a real stock of the kind indicated. Some recipes for stock are given; for any other stocks required you should refer to a general cookery book.

MEDITERRANEAN FISH SOUP

As there is no point in attempting a Bouillabaisse since we do not have the right fish, here is another Mediterranean fish soup from France which we can make successfully. The vital ingredient is saffron, followed by fennel and a dried strip of orange peel – things we can get hold of here. Be sure to buy fish with heads on, and ask the fishmonger if he can give you a collection of sole or turbot bones, skin and heads from filleting white fish (they increase the flavour, improve the texture and cost nothing).

Serves 6

generous 1 kg (2–2½ lb)
    fish – monkfish, conger,
    mullet red or grey,
    gurnard or rascasse
bones and skin
1 large leek, trimmed,
    sliced
1 large onion, quartered
1 medium carrot, sliced
3 large cloves garlic, sliced
outer layer trimmed from a
    fennel bulb, or 2 fennel
    stalks or 2 level
    teaspoons fennel seed

olive oil
bouquet garni
strip of dried orange peel
salt, pepper, cayenne, sugar
large pinch of saffron
dash white wine vinegar
    (optional)
125 ml (4 fl oz) white
    wine, reduced by half
    (optional)
90 g (3 oz) vermicelli or
    other soup pasta

Clean and cut up fish; chop bones into convenient pieces. Put vegetables, garlic and fennel into a huge pan with enough oil to cover the base. Stew with an occasional stir for about 15 minutes, until the onion is soft and yellowing. Put in fish bones, skin, fish, bouquet garni and orange peel. Bring 2 litres (3½ pt) water to the boil and pour it into the pan. Bring rapidly to the boil and boil hard for 15 minutes. Tip into a sieve laid across a large pan. Ignore the more recalcitrant objects —

bones, peel, bouquet, hard bits of fennel. Push through as much of the debris as you feel inclined, to give texture to the soup. Season to taste, adding a pinch of sugar if the flavour needs enhancing. A dash of vinegar or wine can be added too with the same idea.

Bring soup to the boil, tip in the pasta and simmer until it is just cooked. Serve the soup with toasted or baked bread and *rouille*, either to spread on the bread or stir into the soup.

11

CORNMEAL SOUP

SOPA DE MAIZ

Most of the corn that is stored in the *horreos* of Galicia and Asturias goes to feed chickens; some ends up as yellow cornmeal, which is sometimes made into polenta of a porridge consistency; but I prefer it made into this comforting soup from Aragon.

If you cannot get salt cod, use smoked haddock, ideally a good Finnan haddock: it will not taste quite the same, but will be very good. Do not soak it.

Serves 6

250 g (8 oz) salt cod,
  soaked in cold water for
  at least 24 hours
125 g (4 oz) chopped
  onions
60 g (2 oz) diced white
  turnip
bay leaf
grated nutmeg
1 litre (1¾ pt) water

100 g (3½ oz) yellow
  cornmeal
2 cloves of garlic, sliced
4 tablespoons oil
60 g (2 oz) bread, cut
  in cubes
strong meat stock (pages 27
  and 37) or jelly
salt, pepper
chopped parsley

Drain the cod, changing the water twice and put it into a pan with fresh cold water. Bring slowly to simmering point: keep it there until the fish can be flaked easily from the skin and bone, which should be discarded.

Cut the cod up into small pieces. Put into a pan with the vegetables, bay leaf and a good grating of nutmeg plus the water. Bring to simmering point, mix the cornmeal with a little water, then tip it into the soup, stirring well. Cook for 30 minutes on a low heat. Meanwhile, fry the garlic in the oil, putting the pieces of garlic into the soup when they are light brown. Fry the bread, adding extra oil if necessary to serve with the soup.

To improve the flavour add strong meat stock or jelly, season and sprinkle with chopped parsley.

13

BRETON CRAB SOUP

One evening in 1884, Edmond de Goncourt and Émile Zola were invited to dinner by their publisher, Charpentier. It was so delicious that de Goncourt wondered if Charpentier was about to abscond with the cash, and became nervous about money owing on his novel *Chérie*. The star turn was crab soup, a Breton dish little known in Paris at that time. It was like a shellfish bisque, but 'with something finer to it, something tastier, something more of the ocean'.

Serves 6

2 medium-sized cooked
  crabs
sliced carrot
onion stuck with 3 cloves
bouquet garni
250 ml (8 fl oz) dry white
  wine, preferably Muscadet

fish (page 26) or veal or
  chicken stock (page 27)
150 g (5 oz) rice
up to 150 ml (5 fl oz) cream
large knob of butter
salt, pepper, cayenne

Remove the meat from the cooked crabs and set it aside. Put all the debris into a pan with the carrot, onion, *bouquet*, wine and enough stock to cover everything generously. Simmer for 30 minutes. Extract the toughest pieces of claw shell, when whizz the rest in a liquidizer to extract every hint of flavour into the liquid. Pour through a sieve into the rinsed out pan – do not press too hard, just enough to extract the softer part.

In a separate pan meanwhile, cook the rice in some more stock, or water. When very tender, put it into the liquidizer with most of the crab meat (keep enough for the garnish). Blend to a purée and add the crab shell stock. Taste and dilute further if necessary with more stock or water.

Add cream to taste and reheat to just under boiling point. Put in extra seasoning, with a good pinch of cayenne, and the crab pieces you kept for the garnish. Leave for another 5 minutes, still without boiling, then serve with croûtons or bread fried in butter.

SHRIMP AND TOMATO BISQUE

POTAGE À LA CREVETTE

This dish should be made with live shrimps, but if you cannot manage this, use boiled shrimps (or prawns, or mussels opened with white wine).

Serves 6–8

750 g (1½ lb) tomatoes, peeled, chopped
500 g (1 lb) onions, sliced
150–200 g (5–7 oz) shrimps

white wine
salt, pepper, cayenne
a good beef stock (page 37)

Cook tomatoes and onions slowly in a covered pan. When the tomato juices flow, raise the heat and remove the lid. Simmer steadily for about 45 minutes, then sieve.

Meanwhile cover the shrimps generously with white wine, add salt, pepper and cayenne. Bring to the boil, and cook briefly for a moment or two. Try a shrimp to see if it is ready. Strain off the liquid.† Peel the shrimps, setting aside the edible tail part. Put the debris back into the pan with the liquid, and simmer for

15 minutes to extract all flavour from the shells, etc. Strain, pressing as much through as possible. Measure this shrimp liquid, and add an equal quantity both of the tomato purée and beef stock. Bring to the boil, taste for seasoning, and adjust the quantities if you like, adding a little more tomato or stock, or both. A pinch of sugar will help bring out the flavour, if the tomatoes were not particularly good.

Put the shrimp meats into the liquid, and heat for a moment, then serve. Do not keep the soup waiting, as this will toughen the shrimp tails.

Note: if you use cooked shrimps or prawns, start their preparation at †, covering the debris very generously with white wine.

CHILLED GUMBO BISQUE

The gumbo stews of the southern states of America are often given their defining character by okra. Here is a delicious soup in which they may seem subdued: nonetheless they are essential to the satin smoothness and unusual flavour of the soup. This recipe is an anglicized version of a bisque devised by a New York friend to use up a can of crab claws. I never find canned shellfish satisfactory – it is almost as tasteless as the frozen kind – and prefer to use fresh prawns in their shells, or fresh crab claws which are sometimes sold separately. The important thing is to have some hard debris to flavour the stock, as well as soft meat for finishing the soup.

Serves 6

300–350 g (10–12 oz)
prawns in their shells, or
fresh boiled crab claws
1 litre (1¾ pt) fish or
chicken stock (pages 26 or
27), plus ½ litre (15 fl
oz) water or 1 kg (2 lb)
fish trimmings plus 1½
litres (2½ pt) water and
¼ litre (8 fl oz)
dry white wine or cider

100 g (3½ oz) chopped
celery
100 g (3½ oz) chopped
onion
½ green pepper, chopped
2–3 tablespoons butter
250 g (8 oz) okra
1 medium can tomatoes
(approx. 400 g, 14 oz)
100 g (3½ oz) rice
salt, pepper, cayenne

Shell the prawns or crab claws. Put the debris into a large pan. Set aside the meat. To the pan, add the stock and water, or fish trimmings, water and wine or cider. Simmer for 45 minutes to extract the flavours, then strain into a measuring jug and add water to make 1½ litres (2½ pt). Meanwhile soften the celery, onion and pepper in the butter.

Prepare and cut the okra into slices 1 cm (½ in) thick. Add them with the stock, tomatoes and rice to the vegetables. Season. Cover and simmer for an hour. Purée in the blender, dilute further if you like, then chill overnight or for at least 4 hours.

Serve with some or all of the prawn or crab meat.

COD AND SHELLFISH CHOWDER

A most satisfying dish when everyone is tired at the end of the day. Don't despise the frozen packs of cod or haddock on sale in the grocery, they do nicely for chowders; so do frozen scallops or prawns if clams and fresh mussels aren't available.

Serves 6

125 g (4 oz) salt belly of pork or streaky bacon, diced
175–250 g (6–8 oz) chopped onion
1 tablespoon lard or butter
1 heaped tablespoon plain flour
450 ml (15 fl oz) water or fish stock (page 26)
450 ml (15 fl oz) milk
bouquet garni, including a bay leaf

6 medium potatoes, diced
salt, mace, freshly ground pepper, cayenne
750 g (1½ lb) cod or other firm white fish
150 ml (5 fl oz) cream
at least 125 g (4 oz) shelled mussels, clams, scallops, etc.
parsley and chives for garnish

Brown pork (or bacon) and onion lightly in the fat. Stir in the flour and cook for a couple of minutes. Add the water or fish stock gradually, then add the milk, bouquet, and potatoes. Season well with salt, mace and peppers.

When the potatoes are almost cooked, put in the cod, cut into rough 2½ cm (1 in) pieces. After

5 minutes, stir in the cream and shellfish (and any liquor from opening mussels, etc). When the soup returns to the boil remove from the heat. Remember that the cod continues to cook in the heat of the chowder as it comes to table, and should not be over-cooked – neither should the shellfish. Correct the seasoning and sprinkle with parsley and chives.

Hot buttered toast or hot crackers usually accompany a chowder: ship's biscuits if you can get them.

Note: curry powder can be added with the flour. Final garnishes can include sweet red pepper or sweetcorn. Every town on the East Coast has its own small variations.

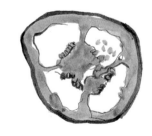

CATALAN MUSSEL SOUP

Serves 6

*1 kg (2 lb) mussels,
scrubbed and scraped
150 g (5 oz) onion, chopped
3 tablespoons olive oil
375 g (12 oz) tomatoes,
peeled, roughly chopped*

*up to 450 ml (15 fl oz)
light fish stock (page 26)
or water
2 large cloves garlic, halved
3 good sprigs parsley
90 g (3 oz) bread, toasted
3 tablespoons brandy
½ teaspoon ground
cinnamon
salt, pepper*

To open the mussels: have ready a colander set over a basin to take the mussels as they are opened. Turn the heat on your hob to very high. Take a wide heavy sauté pan and put in a close single layer of mussels. Put on the lid. Set over the heat and leave for 30 seconds. Check to see if the mussels are open. Remove any that are, put back the lid and

leave for another 10 seconds. The point is to give the mussels the minimum time possible over the heat (ignore cookery book instructions suggesting 2 minutes or even longer: this is unnecessary if you open the mussels in single layer batches). When all are opened, remove and cook the next and subsequent batches. Finally strain the mussel liquor through doubled muslin or other cloth to remove the sandy grit and mud.

Meanwhile, stew the onions in the oil until golden. Add the tomatoes and bubble them for a few minutes before pouring in the mussel liquor and 300 ml (10 fl oz) fish stock or water.

Put the garlic, parsley, bread, brandy and cinnamon into a processor or blender and reduce to crumbs. Add to the soup which it will thicken. Dilute, according to taste, with the remaining stock or water. Correct the seasoning. Add the mussels to the soup, and serve.

OYSTER SOUP

This is the most delicate of fish soups, and is the easiest of all to make. Until oysters become cheap again, you might prefer to substitute mussels, clams or cockles. (This is not a bad joke: with modern methods of fish farming, oysters will be large, plentiful and less expensive before many years have passed.)

Serves 6

*2 dozen oysters or 1 kg
(2 lb) shellfish
60 g (2 oz) butter
2 tablespoons plain flour
600 ml (20 fl oz) hot milk
or veal stock*

*¾ teaspoon anchovy essence
nutmeg, cayenne pepper
150 ml (5 fl oz) double
cream
salt, pepper
lemon juice, parsley*

Clean and open the oysters or other shellfish in the usual way. Discard the shells, but keep the liquor carefully.

Melt the butter in a large pan, stir in the flour and cook gently for 2 or 3 minutes. Add the milk or stock gradually so that the mixture remains smooth. Season with the anchovy essence and a little nutmeg and cayenne. Put in the cream. Simmer for 15–30 minutes. Just before serving, add the oysters and their liquor to the pan to heat through. (Don't overcook shellfish, they become tough; oysters are ready when they *start* to curl at the edges.) Correct the seasoning with salt, pepper, and more nutmeg and cayenne if you like. If the flavour is not quite sharp enough, lemon juice will bring it out. Pour the soup into a hot bowl, scatter a little parsley on top and don't wait for the dilatory guest to appear because the shellfish will go on cooking in the heat of the soup.

AVGOLEMONO SOUP

The name means egg and lemon, which are the two important finishing ingredients of this soup. It's usually made with chicken stock – but try using fish stock as they often do in Greece. Most fishmongers are delighted to hand over free plaice bones, or cheap fish pieces. Avgolemono has a light foamy texture, particularly agreeable on warm days.

Serves 6

FOR THE STOCK
¾–1 kg (1½–2 lb) fish
   bones and pieces
1¾ litres (3 pt) water
150 ml (5 fl oz) wine
   vinegar

medium onion, stuck with
   4 cloves
medium carrot, sliced
8 peppercorns
½ bay leaf, sprig of thyme
   and parsley

Simmer together for 30 minutes. Strain and reduce to about 1½ litres (2½ pt). Correct the seasoning.

TO FINISH THE SOUP
60–90 g (2–3 oz) rice

3 eggs
1–2 lemons

Simmer the rice in the stock until cooked. Have ready in a bowl the eggs beaten up with the juice of 1 lemon. Add a ladleful of hot soup, whisking all the time. Return to the pan, and *without boiling*, cook until slightly thickened. Keep whisking. Add more lemon juice to taste. Serve at once.

CHICKEN STOCK

Makes around ¾ litre (1½ pt)

The carcass and, if available, giblets (not liver) and scraps of skin from 1 chicken
1 onion, quartered
1 carrot, sliced

2 sticks of celery, sliced
1 bay leaf
3 stalks of parsley
1 sprig of thyme
6 black peppercorns

Place all the ingredients in a large pan and cover generously with water. Bring to the boil and simmer for 2–3 hours, occasionally skimming off any scum that rises to the top. Add extra boiling water if the level drops severely. Strain and cool. If you have time, chill in the fridge and lift off any fat that rises and sets on the surface.

MOURTAYROL

CHICKEN AND SAFFRON SOUP

A Languedoc soup made with the liquor of a boiled fowl and thickened with bread sauce, a bread sauce that is yellow with saffron. Any chicken stock you have will do.

Serves 6

1½ litres (2½ pt) well-flavoured chicken stock (page 27)
a generous pinch of saffron filaments

125 g (4½ oz) crust-free bread, sliced
2 tablespoons fruity olive oil
salt, pepper

Heat 150 ml (5 fl oz) of the stock and pour it on to the saffron, in an ovenproof bowl. Leave at least 20 minutes.

Toast the bread lightly, break it up and add it to the saffron liquor. Pour on 200 ml (7 fl oz) more stock. Cover and cook gently in the oven for an hour at Gas mark 2, 150°C (300°F), or on top of the stove like bread sauce. Stir this mixture, which is the *mourtayrol* that gives its name to the soup, and add more stock from time to time. When it is a thick, soft, yellow sauce, stir in the oil and seasoning.

Reheat the rest of the stock and season; divide between the soup bowls. The sauce is passed separately so that each person can take a spoonful (or more, according to taste) and stir it into the stock.

MULLIGATAWNY SOUP

Serves 4–6

*1 boiling fowl, or the
drumstick and thigh
joints of a roasting bird,
plus giblets (frozen
chickens are no good at all
for this recipe)
2 onions, sliced
90 g (3 oz) butter*

*curry powder to taste
175–250 g (6–8 oz) full
fat fromage frais or
1 pot yoghurt
salt
4 cloves
juice of 1 large lemon
boiled rice*

Cut the chicken into pieces. Brown the onions in 60 g (2 oz) of butter with the chicken. Stir in the curry, *fromage frais* or yoghurt and some salt, and stew for a little while so that the juices turn to a brownish crust on the bottom of the pan. They should not burn, so this needs watching. Pour in 1¾ litres (3 pt) of water, and leave to cook. Melt the remaining butter in a little pan with the cloves. After a few minutes you will be able to crush them down with a wooden spoon. Pour in the lemon juice, mix it all up well and tip into the large pan of soup.

Stew for an hour or more depending on the age and toughness of the chicken: the soup is ready when the meat parts easily from the bones, which can then be removed and thrown away. Correct the seasoning, pour into a tureen and serve with a separate bowl of boiled rice.

This mulligatawny soup, unlike some of the other recipes, contains no apple, but if you like you can always serve a dish of chopped apple sprinkled with lemon juice to be added to the soup with the rice.

TURKEY AND HAZELNUT SOUP

Serves 4–6

1½ litres (2½ pt) turkey
 stock
250 g (8 oz) raw turkey
 breast, minced
1 large egg yolk
125 ml (4 fl oz) cream
fresh or dried chervil

½ teaspoon paprika
salt, freshly ground black
 pepper
90 g (3 oz) grilled, chopped
 hazelnuts
60 g (2 oz) butter

Bring the stock to the boil with the turkey breast in it, and simmer for 3 or 4 minutes. Do not allow the turkey to overcook and become rubbery. Liquidize the soup and then sieve it into a clean pan.

Whisk the egg and cream together, pour in a ladleful of soup, still whisking, and return the whole thing to the pan. Stir over a moderate heat until the soup thickens slightly, but do not allow it to boil. Add the remaining ingredients away from the heat, adjusting the seasonings to your own taste.

Toasted almonds, or peeled boiled chestnuts, both roughly chopped, can be substituted for hazelnuts. At Christmas time, use cooked turkey if you like – for instance, the thigh, which may still be slightly pink – and simmer it for a few moments only so that it is thoroughly reheated but no more.

LAMB AND LEEK BROTH

Serves 6

125 g (4 oz) pearl barley,
 soaked 4 hours
1 kg (2 lb) scrag end of
 neck of lamb, sliced
200 g (7 oz) diced carrot
150 g (5 oz) diced turnip

1 small stalk celery,
 chopped
salt, pepper, sugar
2 leeks, trimmed, chopped
chopped parsley

Drain the barley and put it with the lamb into a large pot, with 2 litres (3½ pt) water. Simmer for one hour. Add the next three items with seasoning and a pinch of sugar. Simmer for 1–1½ hours until the meat is cooked. Take out the pieces, discard the bones, and, if you like, the fattiest parts. Skim the surface fat from the soup. Return the pieces of meat to the soup, reheat and add the leeks. Serve 5 minutes later, sprinkled with parsley. Serve with wholemeal bread and butter as a meal in itself.

POTÉE D'AUVERGNE

Cabbage soup is a favourite item of peasant food in southern France, particularly in the central and south-western part that curves from Atlantic to Mediterranean above the Pyrenees. *Potées, garbures* and *soupes aux choux* are enriched with collections of cured pork joints and various devices to enrich the basic mixture of cabbage, potato and water.

Indeed the two words, cabbage soup, may cover few or many ingredients. This list of ingredients gives you an idea of the kind of thing you put in, but remember that you can vary it as you like. All these things are stewed in a large pot slowly for several hours, from 2 to 4 hours according to the housewife's convenience and the heat of her stove. They make an ideal farm lunch, as everything can be pushed into the pot at breakfast time, with water to cover generously, and be left to stew gently without supervision until half an hour before the midday meal, when special details may be added, such as *farcis* or the sausages and potatoes. A modern solid fuel stove or oil-fired cooker is ideal for this kind of dish; it can stew on top or in the oven.

When mealtimes comes, the soup with a little of the vegetable will be drunk first, sometimes thickened with slices of bread and flavoured with a little grated cheese. After that the meat and the main of the vegetables will be eaten, together with the rolls of *farci* or the maize meal dumplings known as *misques*.

Serves 6

750 g (3 lb) bacon hock
half a pig's head, salted or fresh
500 g (1 lb) salt pork, preferably spare rib chops or loin chops
2 firm green cabbages, or 1 large one
500 g (1 lb) carrots, sliced

4 small turnips, diced
½ root celeriac, diced, or 3 stalks celery, chopped
bouquet garni
salt, pepper, grated nutmeg
4 potatoes, preferably Desirée, sliced
smoked sausages or one long smoked sausage

If the salt meat is likely to be very salty, soak it in tepid water for a couple of hours, or overnight if the cure was a long one. The average salted meat in shops in this country should need no soaking.

Slice and blanch the cabbage for 5 minutes in boiling water, then drain. Put meat and cabbage into a big pot, cover with boiling water generously, add the other vegetables, bouquet and simmer for at least 2 hours.

Half an hour before the soup is to be served, put in the potatoes and sausage.

CAWL

(PRONOUNCED 'COWL')

Cawl may mean no more than soup in Welsh, but as you can see it is more than an elegant mouthful or two as a prelude to a main course. It is soup on the grand peasant scale from the old days of fireplace cookery, a meal in itself.

Serves 6–8

beef dripping or bacon fat
1 kg (2 lb) brisket of beef
(or shin, or smoked
gammon, or ham, or 1 lb
each beef and smoked
bacon)
2 large onions
2 or 3 carrots, parsnips,
swede, turnips (quantities
can be varied according to
supply)

2 stalks celery, chopped
bouquet garni
500 g (1 lb) potatoes
(preferably new)
1 small white cabbage,
sliced
2 or 3 leeks
marigold flowers

Melt the fat in a heavy pan and brown first the meat, then the onions, carrots, parsnips, swede, turnip. Transfer everything to a large pan or casserole when it is nicely browned. Cover with cold water to within 4 cm (1½ in) of the rim of the pan; add a little salt and the chopped celery. Bring slowly to the boil, taking off the scum as it rises. Season with bouquet garni, sea salt and freshly ground black pepper. Transfer to a very low heat and leave to simmer for several hours. The friend from whom I had this recipe says that if the heat is gentle enough, the cawl can be left all day or overnight.

Put the potatoes into the pot half an hour before serving (old potatoes should be cut to new potato size), and the cabbage 10 minutes before serving. Chop

the leeks finely, but keep them to one side.

To serve, slice the meat and put it into individual bowls with some of the vegetables and some of the soup. Sprinkle the chopped leeks on top – they will be cooked enough by the time the bowls are on the table – and float a marigold flower in each bowl. Ideally the bowls should either be wooden, or flowery Welsh earthenware.

COCK-A-LEEKIE

An old and distinguished dish of Scottish cookery, dating back at least to the sixteenth century. To me, prunes are what make the soup, the fourth element, the dark accent that pulls the whole thing together both in look and flavour.

Serves 10

*1 kg (2 lb) shin of beef
or 2 litres (4 pt) beef stock
(page 37)
1 capon or large roasting
bird*

*1–1½ kg (2–3 lb) leeks,
trimmed and washed
18 prunes, soaked
salt, pepper*

If you are using beef, put it into a large pot with 2 litres (4 pt) water, bring slowly to the boil, skin and simmer for 2 hours. Put in the bird, plus half the leeks tied in a bundle. Bring back to the boil and simmer for ¾ hour.

If you are using beef stock, start the chicken in the heated stock, with the leeks in a bundle.

Add the prunes. Continue simmering until the chicken and beef are tender – about 30 more minutes. Remove the beef and chicken and put in the rest of the leeks, sliced, cooking them 1–2 minutes.

Serve a slice each of beef and chicken with their broth in a soup plate with prunes and some of the barely cooked leeks (discard the bundle), saving the rest of the meat for a cold meal next day. Or strain off the liquor and serve with a little fresh leek as soup, with the hot meats, prunes and leeks remaining as a main course.

BEEF STOCK

200 g (6 oz) shin of beef,
    minced
300 g (10 oz) beef bones,
    chopped into large pieces
1 large carrot, chopped
1 large onion, chopped
1 large parsley root,
    chopped

125 g (4 oz) celeriac,
    chopped, or 2 stalks celery
butter
sugar, pepper, salt
bouquet garni

Put meat and bones into a pan with 2½ litres (good 4 pt) water. Mix the vegetables together and add half to the pan. Brown the rest lightly in butter, sprinkling on a teaspoon of sugar as they begin to colour. This produces a richer tone and flavour. Add to the pan of meat, swilling out the brown parts if necessary with some of the water from the pan. Season and put in the bouquet. Bring to the boil, skim and simmer, covered, for one to two hours. Strain. (A second weaker stock can be made by pouring more water on the debris and simmering it again.)

PEA AND HAM SOUP

Peas and ham, smoked ham especially, are a wonderful combination, either as a main course, or cooked together in soup. This recipe solves the familiar summer problem of how to use up peas which looked fine in the shop, but turn out to be older and dryer than one thought:

Serves 6

90 g (3 oz) chopped onion
*90 g (3 oz) smoked
  gammon rashers and 1¼
  litres (2 pt) water, or
  90 g (3 oz) diced potato
  and 1¼ litres (2 pt)
  smoked ham stock*
60 g (2 oz) butter
250 g (8 oz) shelled peas
nutmeg, salt, black pepper
1 egg yolk
5 tablespoons double cream

Melt the onion and gammon, or onion and potato, in the butter for 10 minutes over a low heat. Add water, or stock, and peas and seasoning. Simmer until the peas are cooked, then liquidize or put through the *mouli-légumes*. Return to the cooking pan through a strainer and reheat.

When the soup is just under the boil, pour a ladleful on the egg yolk and cream, beaten together in a basin. Put the soup back into the pan and stir over a low heat, without boiling, for 5 minutes until the soup thickens a little more. Correct the seasoning before serving.

YELLOW PEA SOUP

GULÄRTSOPPA/ARTER MED FLÄSK

Yellow pea soup is claimed as a national dish by both Denmark and Sweden. There is no one correct recipe – a Swedish friend said to me briskly, 'The poor add sausage to their yellow peas, the rich smoked bacon and pork.' So take your choice, a smoked pork item of some kind is all that you need.

Danes serve dark rye bread, lager and schnapps with their pea soup (*gule aerter*). The Swedes drink a glass of hot Punsch, their sweet rum-based liqueur, with their pea soup and follow up with pancakes and waffles. Ginger rather than thyme can be the flavouring, with more or less of the other vegetables than the peas, which may or may not be sieved.

Serves 8

300 g (10 oz) yellow split peas, soaked
2½ litres (4½ pt) water
500 g (1 lb) piece of smoked or green streaky bacon, or salt pork
small celeriac, peeled and diced, or 4 stalks of celery, chopped
3 leeks, trimmed and sliced, or 2 bunches of spring onions, trimmed and cut up

250 g (8 oz) peeled, diced carrots
500 g (1 lb) peeled, diced potatoes
6–8 small onions, peeled
6–8 gammon chops, green or smoked
bouquet of thyme sprigs, or level teaspoon powdered ginger
boiling sausage and/or 4 frankfurters

Cook the peas slowly in 1 litre (2 pt) water, without salt, until very tender (about 1½–2 hours). Sieve or process if you like, then season. Meanwhile, simmer the piece of bacon or pork in the remaining water for 2 hours, adding the vegetables after an hour, and the chops, thyme or ginger and boiling sausage, if using, after 1¼ hours.

Remove the bacon or pork,

the chops and boiling sausage, cut them as appropriate and keep warm. Stir the pea purée into the bacon pan, and add extra water if the soup is too thick for your taste. Correct the seasoning. Heat, adding frankfurters 5 minutes before serving soup.

Ladle out the soup, then, as people finish, bring in the meat to eat on side plates, with a second helping of soup.

PEA SOUP

Soup made with fresh peas in the summer and dried peas in winter was a standby of middle-class households in the past. When Jane Austen wrote that she was not ashamed to ask an unexpected visitor – their doctor – to sit down with them and share the dinner, the menu was pease soup, a spare-rib of pork and a pudding. Incidentally, this shows that the huge meals recorded by Parson Woodforde and drawn in diagrams in the cookery books of the time were for dinner parties; when families ate on their own, the meals were very much like our own today. With frozen peas, we can make a fresh-flavoured soup all winter long.

Serves 6–8

*generous ½ litre (¾–1 pt)
shelled mature peas (or
frozen peas)
½ large cucumber,
unpeeled, sliced
heart of a crisp lettuce,
preferably Cos, shredded
small handful of spinach,
shredded (optional)*

*175 g (6 oz) chopped onion
3 sprigs mint
60 g (2 oz) butter
salt, pepper, cayenne
heaped tablespoon each
chopped parsley and
mint
a teacupful young green
peas*

Cook the peas in plenty of water until tender. Meanwhile, in another pan, covered, stew the cucumber, lettuce, spinach, onion and mint sprigs in butter until they are cooked; do this slowly, so that the vegetables do not brown.

Liquidize the peas. Return them to their pan. Then liquidize the vegetables in butter, and add to the peas. Stir in more water to get the consistency you prefer. Season. Add the chopped herbs and the young peas which have been separately cooked. Reheat gently.

ONE-EYED BOUILLABAISSE
WITH PEAS

BOUILLABAISSE BORGNE AUX PETIS POIS

The idea of the title seems to be that when you are too poor or low to afford the fish deemed necessary for bouillabaisse, you make do with vegetables and eggs. You will notice that this humble version of the famous Provençal soup needs the same fast boiling to bring oil and water together. It makes an appetizing lunchtime dish. As leeks are difficult to buy in this country in the summer, use a small bunch of spring onions instead with an ordinary onion.

Serves 6

6 tablespoons olive oil
2 leeks, or spring onions
  and an onion, or a leek
  and an onion, chopped
2 large tomatoes, skinned,
  chopped
4 cloves garlic, crushed
1 sprig garden fennel
finger-length strip of dried
  orange peel

pinch of saffron filaments
6 new potatoes, scraped and
  sliced
500 g (1 lb) shelled peas
salt, pepper
1 egg per person
1 slice stale French bread
  per person
chopped parsley

Heat the oil in a large saucepan and brown the leeks or spring onions and onion very lightly. Put in the tomato, aromatics and potatoes, stirring them well together. Add 2 litres (3½ pt) boiling water. Set over the fiercest, reddest heat you can contrive. When the liquid bubbles hard, put in the peas – choose middle-sized peas of good quality for this recipe, rather than young ones. Add seasoning. Boil hard until the potatoes are almost cooked, then lower the heat and poach the eggs in the soup. Check the seasoning.

Put the bread into individual soup bowls. Remove the eggs and vegetables with a pierced ladle to a serving dish and sprinkle them with parsley. Pour the soup into the bowls. Serve everything together if you like, in the French style, or keep vegetables and eggs warm while you drink the soup.

DRIED MUSHROOM SOUP

GRIBNOI SUP IZ SUSHONNYKH GRIBOV

Dried mushrooms may seem quite expensive, but a few go a remarkably long way. This is a Russian recipe.

Serves 6

*60 g (2 oz) dried
mushrooms, e.g. porcini
from Italian delicatessens
generous 2 litres (3½ pt)
salted water
100 g (4 oz) pearl barley*

*4 potatoes, peeled and cut into cubes
4 carrots, peeled and
coarsely grated
1 onion, peeled and finely chopped
60 g (2 oz) butter
6 tablespoons soured cream*

Wash the mushrooms in warm water. Then boil them for 30–40 minutes in the measured salted water. Remove the mushrooms from the liquid with a draining spoon, chop them and set aside.

Add the pearl barley to the mushroom liquid, and begin to cook it. Add the potatoes and carrots to the mushroom liquid. Meanwhile, fry the onion and the mushrooms in the butter in a frying pan. When the onions are soft and golden, add them and the mushrooms, together with the buttery juices, to the soup. The soup should have been allowed to cook for about 30 minutes from when the pearl barley was added, to the final stage when the fried mushrooms and onions are added to it.

To serve, put a spoonful of soured cream into each person's soup bowl, then ladle in the hot soup.

LENTIL AND APRICOT SOUP

Apricot gives an unidentifiable tartness to an otherwise earthy lentil soup which makes it particularly successful when served cold. My daughter introduced me to this recipe – she finds that with the differing sharpness of apricots, you need to make adjustments in quantity, and that an extra half litre of stock lightens the consistency.

I have allowed for all this, but these are points to watch for.

Serves 8

200 g (7 oz) brown or grey lentils
175 g (6 oz) plump dried apricots or 125 g (4 oz) sharp, dried apricots, soaked, or 6 fresh apricots, stoned
1 tablespoon olive oil
1 medium onion, chopped
1 clove garlic, crushed
1½ litres (3 pt) chicken stock (page 27)
seeds of 6 cardamom pods
salt, pepper
150 ml (¼ pt) cream or yoghurt
chopped coriander leaves, or parsley, or chives

Pick over the lentils and cut apricots into large pieces. In a large pan soften onion in the oil, add garlic and stir for a minute. Put in lentils, apricots, two-thirds of the stock and the crushed cardamom seeds. Simmer for 45–60 minutes. Liquidize or process the mixture, then sieve (always prudent with lentils, as they contain invisible pieces of grit). Season as required. Either reheat with cream or stir in yoghurt and chill, adding extra stock to lighten the consistency. Just before serving, mix in the herbs.

47

TUSCANY BEAN SOUP

The people of Tuscany are the great bean-eaters, the *mangiafagioli*, of Europe. They have so many bean dishes that I'm surprised they've never invented any bean cakes, or buns, in the Japanese style. But they have invented a special pot for cooking beans in, a *fagiolara*. Apart from being a beautiful object, the *fagiolara* is practical: it can be used over low, direct heat, or in the oven, and, on account of its chianti-flask shape, the top is easily sealed against loss of heat and flavour. In these pots, beans simmer in water seasoned with olive oil, garlic, sage, tomato, and perhaps some pickled pork, to make Tuscan – not Boston – baked beans. But for a small party of tired urban stomachs this is the Tuscan recipe I would choose:

Serves 6

250 g (½ lb) dried haricot,
  or butter beans
1¼ litres (2 pt) water
5 or 6 large tablespoons
  olive oil

2 large cloves garlic,
  chopped not crushed
a bunch of parsley, chopped
salt, black pepper

Soak, then simmer the beans in the water *without salt* until cooked. When they are soft, remove a quarter to half of the beans, and liquidize or *mouli* the rest. Season well, diluting the soup with more water if necessary. Reheat, with the whole beans. In a separate pan cook the garlic slowly in 2 tablespoons of the olive oil, until it turns golden. Add to the soup, with the parsley and the rest of the oil. Serve immediately.

Note: if you can't buy good olive oil, don't make do with corn oil, which is tasteless. Use butter instead. The result will be quite different, more like a French soup, but still very good.

TOMATO AND HARICOT BEAN OR LENTIL SOUP

This tomato soup is full of flavour and interest and particularly restoring in summer when the heat dies down and everyone feels tired. The ideal is to use a richly flavoured variety of tomatoes from the garden, and to serve the soup with a thick scatter of chopped basil leaves. If you have to substitute parsley and chives, for instance in wintertime, use butter rather than olive oil as the cooking fat.

Serves 6

*125 g (4 oz) haricot beans
 or lentils
100 g (3 oz) smoked
 streaky bacon or
 geräuchter* bauchspeck
125 g (4 oz) chopped onion

*1 small stem celery,
 chopped, or celery leaves
1 large clove garlic, chopped
3–4 tablespoons olive oil
 (or butter) 500 g (1 lb)
 peeled, chopped tomatoes
 or 400 g (14 oz) can
2 tablespoons tomato
 concentrate or ketchup
1 litre (2 pt) beef stock
 (page 37)
salt, pepper, brown sugar
chopped basil, or parsley
 and chives
bread cubes fried in olive oil
 or butter*

Put the dried vegetables in a basin and pour over enough boiling water to cover them by a good 2½ cm (1 in). Leave for an hour or two until they begin to soften. Cook the bacon, onion, celery and garlic gently in the oil or butter, in a covered pan so that they do not brown. Add the beans or lentils and their water, and tomatoes, concentrate or ketchup and stock. Simmer untill the dried vegetables are cooked. Now add salt, plenty of pepper and sugar if necessary. Simmer for three minutes. Purée half the soup in a blender, then pour it back into the pan – this makes a slightly thickened but

not too heavy soup; if you need to, dilute it further with more stock or water. Reheat and correct the seasoning. Scatter with herbs and serve with the bread cubes.

RED ONION AND WINE SOUP

Start by making a herb stock, which can be done 1–2 hours in advance. Simmer together, for 25 minutes, 1¾ litres (3¼ pt) water and 1 scant teaspoon of salt with several branches of fresh thyme or 1 teaspoon dried thyme, 8 branches parsley, 3 bay leaves, 3 cloves of garlic, all tied into a muslin. Finally, remove the bag, squeezing out the liquid, and keep until required.

Serves 8–10

1 kg (2 lb) red onions
a well-flavoured olive oil
4 cloves garlic, chopped
½ teaspoon coarse salt

500 g (1 lb) can chopped
tomatoes, plus 2 or 3 fresh
tomatoes, skinned, seeded
and chopped
250 ml (8 fl oz) Beaujolais
or other full-bodied red
wine
salt, pepper
2–3 slices of baguette per
person, or thick slices of a
more interesting bread
fresh thyme leaves

If the onions are large, quarter them. If medium to small, cut them in thirds. Then slice thinly. Stir them in a large soup pot with 4–5 tablespoons olive oil over a low heat. When they are coated, leave to stew down slowly, about 30 minutes in all, stirring occasionally.

Pound the garlic with the coarse salt, then stir it into the soft onions with all the tomato and about a mugful of the herb stock. Add ½ teaspoon salt, cover and stew 15 minutes. Add the wine and boil it vigorously without a lid to reduce to a slack purée. Pour in the remaining stock, half cover and leave to simmer 25 minutes. Check seasoning, adding pepper.

Brush the bread with oil and bake until nicely browned in a moderate oven. Put into 8–10 bowls, ladle on the soup. Add a little olive oil to each and sprinkle with fresh thyme.

Alternatively, you could just serve the bread with the soup, or half and half. The slices should end up crisp all through, and thick.

PALESTINE SOUP

Serves 6

*500 g (1 lb) large
  Jerusalem artichokes, or
  250 g (½ lb) each
  artichokes and potatoes
1 large onion, chopped
1 clove garlic, chopped
½ stick celery, chopped*

*125 g (4 oz) butter
2 rashers green back bacon,
  or 60 g (2 oz) ham
1 litre (1¾ pt) light
  chicken or turkey stock
  (page 27), or water
¼ litre (8 fl oz) milk
  (optional)
salt, pepper
6 tablespoons cream
chopped parsley and chives*

Scrub and boil the artichokes in salted water for 5 to 10 minutes, then run them under the tap and remove the peel. I think this is the easiest thing to do, though if you prefer to peel them raw, it doesn't matter. It entirely depends on the shape of the artichokes.

Cut up the artichokes. If you are using potatoes, peel and dice them.

Put them with the onion, garlic and celery in a large pan with half the butter. Cover tightly, and stew over a low heat for ten minutes, giving the pan an occasional shake or stir. Now add the bacon or ham, and cook a moment or two longer. Pour in the stock or water, and leave to simmer until all the vegetables are soft. Blend if you want a smooth soup, or put through the *mouli-légumes* if you like a knobbly texture. Reheat, adding more water, or the milk, to dilute to taste. Correct the seasoning. Finally stir in the last of the butter, the cream and herbs. Serve with croûtons of bread fried in butter.

BEETROOT CONSOMMÉ

Serves 6

1½ litres (2½ pt) clarified
beef, chicken (page 27) or
duck stock
2 large boiled beetroot,
skinned

salt, pepper, lemon juice
150 ml (5 fl oz) soured
cream
chopped parsley and chives

Put the stock into a large pan.
Chop the beetroot and set aside
three heaped tablespoons. Add
the rest of the stock and bring to
just below boiling point. Keep
it at this heat for about half
an hour – it should give an
occasional burp, or show a few
small bubbles, but that is all.

The point being to make an
infusion of the stock and beetroot. Just before serving add the
reserved beetroot to freshen the
colour and leave for a further few
minutes. Strain into a hot tureen,
check the seasoning and add a
little lemon juice. Mix the cream
with the herbs and serve in a separate bowl.

CHILLED BEETROOT SOUP
Follow the recipe for beetroot
consommé, but strain the consommé into individual bowls and
set in the refrigerator to chill. Mix
the cream with the herbs, and
swirl a spoonful of this mixture
into each bowl of soup.

BROAD BEAN SOUP

Serves 6

125 g (4 oz) chopped onion
1 clove garlic, chopped
60 g (2 oz) butter
250 g (1 lb) shelled broad
    beans
2–3 bean pods, black part
    removed

chopped fresh savory, or
    sage, or parsley
salt, pepper, sugar
6 tablespoons double cream
lemon juice, chopped green
    onion stalk

Soften the onion and garlic in butter without letting them colour. Add the beans, 1 litre (1¾ pt) water, the pods and a few sprigs of whichever herb you choose. When the beans are cooked, remove a tablespoon of them and peel off the white skins. Set aside. Sieve or blend the soup. Reheat with the skinned beans, adding more liquid if necessary to dilute the consistency. Season to taste, with a pinch of sugar. Add a little more of the chopped herb, the cream and a few drops of lemon juice to bring out the flavour, then the onion stalk. Serve with little cubes of bread fried in butter.

CELERIAC SOUP

The unusual idea of combining celeriac and dried ceps is East European. If you cannot buy dried Polish ceps at the delicatessen, Italian *funghi porcini* will do just as well as they are the same mushroom (though they tend to be more expensive). If you dry your own, you will have no trouble.

Serves 6

15 g (½ oz) dried ceps
100 g (3–4 oz) prepared celeriac, chopped
100 g (3–4 oz) chopped onion
60 g (2 oz) butter

150 ml (5 fl oz) each soured and single cream
1 level tablespoon flour
chopped dill weed or parsley
salt, pepper

Pour a ladleful of very hot water over the ceps, and leave them to soak for 20–30 minutes. Sweat the celeriac and onion meanwhile in the butter, in a covered pan, until they begin to soften, then add the mushrooms and their liquor. Simmer, covered, until the vegetables are tender. Purée in a blender, or put through the *mouli-légumes*, and return the purée to the pan. Mix the creams with the flour to make a smooth paste and stir into the soup as it reheats. Cook slowly for about 5 minutes, until the taste of flour has gone. If the soup is too thick for you – it may be if it was blended – dilute with more water. Stir in chopped dill weed to taste, or parsley, and seasoning. Serve with croûtons.

DANISH CELERY AND CHEESE SOUP

A number of good soups can be made with celery, but this is the most delicious of them all. The creamed blue cheese gives a savoury yet tactful richness to the light flavour of celery. If you are using a milder blue cheese than the Danish kind, be prepared to add extra.

Serves 6

*1 medium head celery,
   chopped fairly small*
2 medium onions, chopped
*50 g (scant 2 oz) lightly
   salted butter*
30 g (1 oz) plain flour

*1 litre (2 pt) chicken stock
   (page 27)*
salt, pepper
*60 g (2 oz) Danish blue
   cheese*
chopped parsley

Cook the vegetables in the butter for 10 minutes in a covered pan without browning them. Stir in the flour thoroughly, then moisten with the stock. Season. Cover and simmer for 40 minutes, until the celery is really tender. Mash the cheese to a cream and whisk it gradually into the soup just before serving it; once you start doing this, lower the heat to make sure the soup remains well below boiling point. Correct the seasoning, add parsley, and serve with croûtons.

SPANISH PEPPER SOUP

An unusual and spicy soup. One of the best vegetable soups I know, light but full of interest and flavour.

Serves 6

250 g (8 oz) tomatoes, chopped
1 dessertspoon wine or sherry vinegar
1 rounded teaspoon dark brown soft sugar
2 litres (3½ pt) beef stock (page 37)
2 large peppers, grilled, skinned, diced

100–125 g (3–4 oz) green beans, cut in 1 cm (½ in) lengths
3 tablespoons long grain rice
good pinch saffron
small pinch cayenne
1 heaped teaspoon Spanish or other mild paprika
salt, pepper
chopped chervil or parsley

Reduce the tomatoes, vinegar and sugar to a small amount of concentrated purée. Sieve it into a large pan. Add the stock and bring to the boil. Put in the peppers, beans, rice, saffron and seasonings. When the rice is cooked, the soup will be ready.

Correct the seasoning and serve with chervil or parsley scattered on top.

Canned peppers can be used for this soup – though the flavour will not be quite as good; a small can, with 4 peppers, will be needed.

RUSSIAN CUCUMBER AND SORREL SOUP

Serves 6

250 g (½ lb) sorrel
200 ml (7 fl oz) double and
single cream mixed
300 ml (10 fl oz) natural
yoghurt
½ litre (15 fl oz) cold
consommé or beef stock
(page 37)
250 g (½ lb) cucumber,
chopped

3 hard-boiled eggs, chopped
chopped chives
chopped green fennel or
tarragon
salt, pepper
lemon juice

Remove the thickest sorrel stems; rinse and cut up the sorrel with scissors. Put it into a pan with no extra liquid and stir it over a moderate heat until it is reduced to a dark green purée. Put into a big soup tureen and leave to cool. Add the remaining ingredients in the order given, mixing them in well and adjusting the quantities of herbs and seasonings to taste. Serve chilled.

Note: Spinach can be used instead of sorrel, but increase the amount of lemon juice to get the right sharpness.

CURRIED PARSNIP SOUP

Serves 6

1 heaped tablespoon
  coriander seeds
1 level teaspoon cumin seed
1 dried red chilli, or ½
  teaspoon chilli flakes
1 rounded teaspoon ground
  turmeric
¼ teaspoon ground
  fenugreek

1 medium onion, chopped
1 large clove garlic, split
1 large parsnip, peeled, cut
  up
2 heaped tablespoons butter
1 tablespoon flour
1 litre (2 pt) beef stock
  (page 37)
150 ml (¼ pt) cream
chopped chives or parsley

Whizz the first five ingredients in an electric coffee mill, or pound them in a mortar; mix the ground with the unground spices in the mill or mortar, so that they have a chance to blend well together. Put the mixture into a small jar – you will not need it all for this recipe, but can use it up with lentils or spinach.

Cook the onion, garlic and parsnip gently in the butter, lid on the pan, for 10 minutes. Stir in the flour, and a tablespoon of the spice mixture. Cook for 2 minutes, giving the whole thing a turn round from time to time. Pour in the stock gradually. Leave to cook. When the parsnip is really tender, purée in the blender and dilute to taste with water. Correct the seasoning. Reheat, add the cream and serve scattered with chives or parsley. Cubes of bread fried in butter can be served as well.

CREAM OF TURNIP SOUP

At whatever season of the year you are buying turnips, avoid those that look faded or heavily calloused, or that smell strongly. Young white turnips come in round or long shapes; there is little difference between them in flavour. Turnips need to be peeled, after they have been topped and tailed – when young, they need only the thinnest layer removing – and a preliminary blanching, between 5 and 10 minutes.

Serves 6

350 g (12 oz) young
  turnips, diced
250 g (8 oz) potatoes, diced
1 leek or 4 spring onions or
  1 medium onion, chopped
2 tablespoons butter
1 tablespoon plain flour

1½–2 litres (2½–3½ pt)
  stock (pages 27 and 37)
salt, black pepper
2 large egg yolks
4 tablespoons whipping or
  double cream

Cook the vegetables in the butter in a covered pan over a low heat for ten minutes; shake the pan occasionally, or stir the vegetables about – they must not brown. Add the flour, stir again, then moisten gradually with enough stock to cover the vegetables easily. Season and simmer until the vegetables are tender, from 20–30 minutes.

Blend or sieve the soup through the *mouli-légumes*, adding enough of the remaining stock to make an agreeable consistency. Return the soup to the pan and reheat gently.

Mix the yolks and cream, add a ladleful of hot soup, stirring well, then return to the pan and heat through for a few moments without boiling. Keep stirring. Taste again for seasoning. Serve with bread croûtons.

FRENCH BEAN AND ALMOND SOUP

Split almonds fried to an appetizing golden-brown in a little butter make a good garnish for French beans as a vegetable. With a fresh bean soup they are even more successful.

Serves 6

*375 g (12 oz) French
  beans
100 g (3–4 oz) chopped
  onion
1 large clove garlic,
  finely chopped
butter
1 heaped tablespoon flour
1 litre (1¾ pt) water
  or light chicken stock
  (page 27)*

*salt, pepper
½ teaspoon chopped fresh
  summer savory
lemon juice
60 g (2 oz) almonds,
  blanched and split*

66

Top and tail the beans, stringing them if necessary. Cook the onion and garlic gently in 2 tablespoons of butter, without browning them at all. When they are soft, stir in the flour, then just over half the water or stock. Simmer for a few moments, then put in the beans, seasoning and savory. When the beans are just tender – do not overcook them, or you will lose the best of their flavour – purée the soup in a blender. Use the rest of the water or stock, plus extra water, to dilute the soup to the consistency you like. Reheat, adding more seasoning to taste if necessary and a squeeze of lemon juice to bring out the flavour. Keep the soup just below boiling point.

Fry the almonds in a tablespoon of butter, stirring them about until they are nicely browned. Mix into the soup with a little extra knob of butter and serve immediately.

ASPARAGUS SOUP À LA COMTESSE

Serves 6–8

365 g (12 oz) trimmed
  asparagus
125 g (4 oz) butter
60 g (2 oz) flour
600 ml (20 fl oz) chicken
  stock (page 27)

salt, pepper
2 egg yolks
2 tablespoons double cream
pinch sugar
extra knob butter

Parboil the asparagus, then cut off the tips – which will be just tender – and set them aside. Cut the stalks into 1 cm (¼ in) lengths. Stew them in half the butter in a covered pan until they are completely cooked. Meanwhile, in another pan, melt the remaining butter, stir in the flour and then the chicken stock. Simmer, then moisten the asparagus in butter with some of the stock and liquidize. Pour through a strainer (to catch the last few stringy parts of the

asparagus stalk, should there be any). Reheat gently and season.

Beat the yolks with the cream. Pour in a little of the soup, stirring vigorously, then return to the pan. Stir over a moderate heat, without boiling the soup, for 5 minutes; add a pinch of sugar to bring out the flavour, any extra seasoning required, and finally the asparagus tips which should be given time to heat through in the hot soup, and the extra knob of butter.

Note: thawed frozen asparagus can be used instead of fresh. It will not need parboiling. Add the tips to the soup before thickening it with yolks and cream, so that they have a chance of becoming thoroughly tender.

PUMPKIN SOUP

VELOUTÉ AU POTIRON

Pumpkin soups in France are often very simple indeed – a slice of pumpkin cooked and sieved, then diluted with milk and water, plus cream and either salt, pepper and nutmeg or sugar. White wine is drunk with it, and little cubes of golden fried bread set off its creamy orange colour. Here is a general vegetable soup with pumpkin predominating, from the Franche-Comté. If you have no pumpkin, substitute little gem squash, courgettes or Jerusalem artichokes.

Serves 4–6

150 g (5 oz) peeled,
  chopped tomato
60 g (2 oz) chopped onion
250 g (8 oz), diced potatoes
200 g (7 oz) peeled and
  seeded pumpkin
90 g (3 oz) butter
1 litre (1¾ pt) water

60 g (2 oz) tapioca
3 egg yolks
500 ml (15 fl oz)
  whipping cream
1 teaspoon wine vinegar
salt, and pepper, cayenne
pinch of sugar

Stew the vegetables in the butter in a heavy pan for 5–10 minutes, stirring them occasionally and making sure they do not brown. Pour in the water and simmer until the vegetables are tender. Process or put through a *mouli-légumes* into a clean pan. Reheat, stir in the tapioca and simmer for about 20 minutes.

Meanwhile, beat the egg yolks and cream together. Pour in some of the soup, then tip it back into the pan and heat through for a minute or two without boiling. Add the vinegar gradually to sharpen the flavour, and seasonings (the vinegar is to compensate for the blandness of English cream and tomato, but you may not need it, or the sugar).

Serve with toasted bread, covered with thin slices of Comté or Gruyère cheese melted under the grill.

AUBERGINE SOUP WITH
RED PEPPER

The deep pink pepper cream used to garnish this soup also goes well with firm fish and above all with large, very fresh prawns, especially with some cayenne added.

Serves 6–8

1 kg (2 lb) aubergines
1 medium red pepper
1 medium red onion,
* coarsely chopped*
3 cloves garlic, chopped

4 tablespoons light olive oil
½ litre (scant 2 pt) chicken
* stock (page 27)*
6–8 tablespoons whipping
* cream*

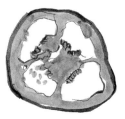

Grill the aubergines and pepper until they are black and blistered. Put the pepper into a cloth or plastic bag while you run the aubergines under the tap and peel away the skins. Then cut them into large dice. Peel the pepper, crush it to a paste and set aside. In a large pan stew the aubergine, onion and garlic with the olive oil for about 20 minutes, until soft. Stir often and do not allow them to brown. Pour on the stock, add seasoning, cover and simmer for 10 minutes. Then liquidize the soup in a blender and return to the pan. Taste for seasoning and bring to just under boiling point.

Meanwhile whip the cream, adding the pepper as it thickens. The end result should stand in soft peaks. Season it. Serve the soup in very hot bowls, with a nice blob of deep pink pepper cream in the middle.

73

CORIANDER SOUP

An easy soup, especially if you use water instead of stock. I confess to preferring it in most vegetable soups: the flavour seems clearer and lighter. But it's a matter of personal preference.

Serves 8

4 medium onions, coarsely chopped
4 tablespoons olive oil
2 cloves of garlic, peeled
4 medium potatoes, peeled and coarsely chopped

1½ litres (2½ pt) good chicken stock (page 27) or water
salt, freshly ground black pepper, cayenne
a large bunch of coriander, chopped

Soften the onions in 3 tablespoons of the oil for about 5 minutes, add the garlic and potatoes and the remaining oil. Stir around for a minute. Add the liquid and simmer until the potato is well cooked. Process or blend in batches, or put through a *mouli-légumes* or sieve. Taste, season and add the coriander. Serve hot with crusty bread or leave to cool and serve chilled.

CARROT SOUP
WITH CHERVIL CREAM

Serves 6–8

4 large shallots, finely chopped
45 g (1½ oz) unsalted butter
1¼ kg (2½ lb) good carrots

1¾–2 litres (3–3½ pt) chicken stock (page 27)
salt, freshly ground black pepper
125 ml (4 fl oz) whipping cream
2–3 tablespoons chopped chervil

Sweat the shallots in the butter over a low heat. Scrape or peel and dice the carrots. Add them to the shallots and stir thoroughly. Continue to cook gently for about 10 minutes, stirring from time to time. Add stock to barely cover the carrots and simmer until tender. Put through a *mouli-légumes*, dilute further to taste and season.

Whip the cream until thick but not stiff. Season and add the chervil to taste.

Reheat the soup without boiling and divide between very hot bowls. Float spoonfuls of the chervil cream on top.

POTATO SOUP

I should think that potatoes are more used than any other vegetable in northern Europe for soups. Apart from their availability, they are so easily varied as a soup flavouring by adding leeks and onions and so on, or by cheese, spices and herbs. In this recipe the additions are lard and garlic, which both blend wonderfully with potato. Instead of the croûtons, or even with them, you could provide a small bowl of crisp bacon pieces.

Serves 6

375 g (12 oz) peeled,
diced potato
100 g (3–4 oz) chopped
onion
2–3 large cloves garlic,
finely chopped

2 big tablespoons lard or
pork fat
1 litre (1¾ pt) light beef
(page 37) or veal stock, or
water
salt, pepper
chopped parsley
cubes of bread fried in lard,
with garlic

Cook the potatoes, onion and garlic in the lard over a gentle heat for about 10 minutes, turning them over occasionally. This process should not be hurried, or the vegetables will brown and the special flavour of garlic and lard will be spoiled. Add the stock or water and simmer until the potato is tender. Sieve or purée in the blender. Reheat the soup and check the seasoning. Stir in the parsley, and serve with the bread in a separate bowl.

SWEETCORN SOUP

The addition of sweet pepper and cayenne spices the mild delicacy of sweetcorn soup; without such assistance, it can – to some people – taste a little too sweet, even sickly. In summer, this recipe makes a delicious chilled soup: keep the hot seasoning for either a *rouille* sauce to go with it or to blend with cream.

Serves 6

250–300 g (8–10 oz) sweetcorn kernels, preferably fresh or frozen, rather than canned
½ litre (generous ¾ pt) veal, beef (page 37) or chicken (page 27) stock
1 small onion, finely chopped
1 tablespoon butter
1 level tablespoon plain flour
½ litre (generous ¾ pt) milk
water
4 tablespoons whipping or double cream
salt, pepper, cayenne
1 red pepper, grilled, skinned, seeded
chopped parsley

Cook the sweetcorn in the stock, then purée it. The mixture will not be completely smooth, but this improves the texture so do not worry about it. If you have no electric blender, put the sweetcorn and stock through the coarse, then the medium, blade of the *mouli-légumes* to get it as fine as possible.

Meanwhile make a béchamel sauce by softening the onion in the butter, then stirring in the flour and finally the milk. Simmer for 5 or 10 minutes gently, then add the sweetcorn and stock purée. Dilute to the consistency you like with water; if the soup is to be chilled, it should not be thick. Stir in the cream and reheat if desired. Season with salt, pepper and cayenne. Dice the pepper fairly small and add to the hot soup just before serving it, with a good sprinkling of parsley. For cold soup, mash the red pepper with some more cream and add a good seasoning of cayenne to make it vigorously hot; alternatively make a *rouille*.

79

WATERCRESS AND POTATO SOUP

Watercress makes one of the best of all soups, whether you make it with potatoes or as a cream soup. The French have long called it *potage de santé*. The name goes back to the eighteenth century – no doubt because watercress was regarded, as Philip Miller said, as a spring tonic against scurvy and to clear the blood, but even more I suspect because of the clean true flavour. If you decide to purée the soup with a blender rather than with a *mouli-légumes*, you can reduce the quantities by about a third.

Serves 6

300 g (10 oz) watercress
350 g (12 oz) potatoes, peeled, cut up
1 medium onion, chopped
60 g (2 oz) butter
¾ litre (1½ pt) water or liquid from green haricot beans
salt, pepper
250 ml (8 fl oz) milk
250 ml (8 fl oz) single or whipped cream

2 egg yolks (optional: see recipe)
chervil if possible, otherwise parsley, chopped

80

Set aside and chop some of the best watercress leaves. Cut up the rest roughly and put with potato and onion into a pan with the butter. Cook gently for 10 minutes, stirring occasionally so that the vegetables become buttery without browning. Add water or bean liquid, salt and pepper, and simmer for about 20 minutes until the potato is cooked. Put through the *mouli-légumes* or blender, and return to the rinsed out pan. If the purée is too thick, add more water along with the milk and the chopped watercress leaves. Bring to just under boiling point and cook for 5 minutes. Beat the cream and yolks together and stir in. Keep over a low heat for a few seconds, so that the flavours blend together. Check the seasoning. Add chervil or parsley and serve.

Note: yolks can be omitted and cream reduced in quantity; if you intend to do this, use a light chicken or veal stock rather than water, to add richness of flavour.

AVOCADO SOUP

SOPA DE AGUACATE

A delicate soup from Mexico, home of the avocado. The only problem is that you cannot keep it hanging around, or you will lose the fine flavour; the avocado cream and stock should be heated together at the last minute. The complementary advantage is that you can produce a first-class soup in minutes, for unexpected visitors.

Serves 6

2 ripe avocados, peeled, stoned
250 ml (8 fl oz) whipping cream, or half single and half double cream

1 litre (1¾ pt) chicken stock (page 27)
1 glass dry or medium sherry parsley, salt, pepper, lemon juice

Reduce the avocados to a purée with the cream. Get it as smooth as possible by using a blender. Heat the stock and pour it on to the cream. Return to the pan and bring to just below boiling point.

Add sherry, chopped parsley and seasoning if required. A very little lemon juice can be used to bring out the flavour.

This soup can be served chilled. Use a light home-made stock, and blend it with the avocado and cream without heating it. Try a seasoning of ground allspice and chilli sauce, with a little sugar. Sprinkle with chopped chives before serving.

APRICOT AND APPLE SOUP

APRIKOS OCH APPEL SOPPA

Serve hot in cold weather, or chilled in summertime.

Serves 8–10

500 g (1 lb) fresh apricots, stoned, or 375 g (12 oz) dried apricots, soaked
1 kg (2 lb) cooking apples, peeled, cored, cut up
2 sticks of celery, halved
small bunch of parsley
bay leaf

1½ litres (2½ pt) light stock (e.g. chicken, page 27)
salt
about 200 ml (7 fl oz) cream
30 g (1 oz) toasted hazelnuts or almonds

Cook the fruit, celery and herbs in the stock for 30 minutes. Remove the celery and herbs and liquidize. Season with salt, stir in the cream and reheat or chill, in either case adding extra stock or water to dilute to the consistency you prefer. Serve scattered with the nuts. Rye biscuits are nice with the soup.

CHESTNUT AND APPLE SOUP

Many European chestnut soups are flavoured with bacon, and made on the heavy side. Understandable, when soup had to be the whole meal. This apple and chestnut recipe is more suitable for soup as a first course only.

Serves 4

500 g (1 lb) chestnuts in
their shells
2 litres (3½ pt) light beef
stock (page 37) or water
1 stick celery heart
2 large Cox's apples, peeled,
cored, sliced

60 g (2 oz) butter
125 g (4 oz) single cream
salt, pepper
bread croûtons fried
in butter

Nick the chestnuts from the centre to the pointed top, at right angles to the base. Boil them in water for 10 minutes, then turn the heat off and remove the chestnuts one by one to peel them. To do this, put your left hand into an open glove to hold the chestnut, then use a small sharp knife to peel off the shell, and then to remove the inner brown skin. If the chestnuts were a good, fat glossy brown to start with, they should be quite easy to deal with. Making a nick from the centre to the pointed end means that the shell peels off much more easily, and the nut in consequence remains more or less intact (though for this recipe, it doesn't matter if the nuts have crumbled into pieces).

Now cook the chestnuts with the stock and celery for about 20 minutes; meanwhile simmer the apple slices in the butter with a good sprinkling of pepper. Liquidize chestnuts, celery and apple with the stock and the buttery apple juices. Taste and correct seasoning. Add the cream. If the soup is too thick for your taste (the thickness will obviously depend on how many chestnuts had to be discarded), dilute it with water. It should not be too heavy in texture, but light, with a faint sharpness from the apples. Serve with croûtons.

STRAWBERRY SOUP

SOUPE AUX FRAISES

Soup for the wrong end of the meal, and soup of a deliciously light
yet thick consistency.

Serves 6

1 kg (2 lb) strawberries
125 g (4 oz) sugar
small wineglass – 100 ml
(3½ fl ox) – red wine

1 rounded teaspoon
* cornflour*
6 tablespoons whipping
* cream*

Remove 6 or 8 of the best strawberries. Hull the rest – they need
not be the finest-shaped strawberries or the biggest, but they
should taste good – and cut up
roughly into a pan. Add the
sugar, and a very little water, just
enough to get things going.
Bring to simmering point, and
as the strawberries begin to give
up their juice, stir in the red wine

mixed with the cornflour. Stir and continue to cook until the strawberries have had 10 minutes simmering in all. Liquidize or process and sieve, or just sieve, into a serving bowl, beating the mixture as it cools from time to time. Taste when cold, adding more sugar or wine as you think fit (strawberries vary and so do people's tastes).

Chill and serve with the best strawberries halved on top and blobs of whipped cream: the consistency should be enough to hold the strawberries and cream so that they are not entirely submerged from view.

WHITE GAZPACHO

Serves 6

60 g (2 oz) blanched
  almonds or pine kernels
4 fat garlic cloves
90 g (3 oz) unbleached
  white bread (weighed
  without crusts)
4 tablespoons olive oil

1 tablespoon white wine
  vinegar
1 teaspoon salt
600 ml (20 fl oz) water
18 white grapes (preferably
  Muscat), skinned,
  halved and pipped

Put the blanched almonds or pine kernels, garlic cloves, peeled and halved, and unbleached white bread into a food processor or blender. Whizz to a paste with a little water. Gradually add the olive oil, then the white wine vinegar and salt.

When blended, slowly pour in about a pint of water to obtain a smooth soup. Add more salt, vinegar and water, according to the seasoning and consistency you prefer.

Chill thoroughly in a large, covered bowl. Serve in individual bowls, adding an ice cube and three skinned, halved and pipped grapes to each bowl.

CATALAN NUT SOUP

Serves 6

60 g (2 oz) hazelnuts,
  toasted and skinned
60 g (2 oz) blanched
  almonds, split
2 cloves of garlic, halved
85 g (3 oz) bread, fried in
  olive oil

1¼ litres (2 pt) light stock
  (e.g. chicken page 27) or
  water
a pinch of saffron strands
salt, pepper

Put the nuts and garlic into a blender. Break up the fried bread and add that, then whizz to crumbs, adding a little of the liquid.

Heat the remaining liquid with the saffron. Add the contents of the blender, bring to simmering point and simmer for 30 minutes. Taste and add salt, pepper and extra liquid as required.

MELON SOUP

A Russian soup so delicate that it makes an ideal first course for a summer party.

Serves 6

*1 melon weighing generous
1 kg (2 lb)
150 g (5 oz) sugar
250 ml (8 fl oz) dry white
wine*

*lemon juice
150–300 ml (5–10 fl oz)
soured cream or crème
fraîche*

Discard pips and scoop the flesh from the melon. Ideally you should have ¾ kg (1½ lb) weight, but do not worry if you have less or more. The other quantities can be adjusted to your taste – and this will depend more on the strength of the melon's flavour than on its bulk.

Dissolve 600 ml (1 pt) water and the sugar in a pan over a low heat, then simmer for 4 or 5 minutes.

Liquidize the melon with the wine, and gradually add the cooled syrup to it. Stop when it tastes right, having regard to the fact that you will be adding a faint sharpener of lemon juice, and at least 150 ml (5 fl oz) cream. More if you like.

As you see, an easy recipe and one that always turns out well. Serve the soup chilled with tiny almond biscuits, or tiny meringues.

INDEX

Index